Advance praise for *Tears in God's Bottle* ...

"*Tears in God's Bottle* is a psalm. It lets us see as God sees. It lets us come to the painful healing that is the consequence of love and our inability to protect our beloveds . . . Many seem to be waiting for God to answer Job, but here is Job's reply—caregiving that brings *our* suffering into the healing of *the* suffering."

—Stephen and Ondrea Levine
Authors of *Who Dies?* and *Embracing the Beloved*

"As those who have been daily caregivers for chronically ill and dying loved ones know, there are hardly adjectives to describe the intensity of the painful emotions experienced. In this book Wayne Ewing, whose wife succumbed to Alzheimer's disease in her sixty-first year, writes of his experience with this terrible process. He is blessed with an articulate and poetic style of writing, a tremendous measure of faith, and a soulful awareness as he tells of the dreadful effects of this illness on the victim and especially on the caregivers—the ones standing by to witness, participate, and maintain their balance as best they can. This book is certain to be inspiring to countless persons in the position of caregiver."

—Nicholas Nossaman, MD
Past president, American Institute of Homeopathy

"Don't be fooled. *Tears in God's Bottle* is not just a book for caregivers. It is a sacred parable of love, commitment, and spiritual triumph that will lift you toward heaven. If you will but read this book, it will nourish your heart forever."

—Hugh Prather
Author of *Spiritual Notes to Myself* and *Notes to Myself*

TEARS IN GOD'S BOTTLE

Tears in God's Bottle

Reflections on Alzheimer's Caregiving

Wayne Ewing

Photographs by Dasha Wright Ewing

With a foreword by Dorothy Ives

WhiteStone Circle Press
Tucson, Arizona

Published by: WhiteStone Circle Press
1718 East Speedway Boulevard, Suite 319
Tucson, AZ 85719

Editor: Ellen Kleiner
Book design and typography: Richard Harris
Cover design and production: Christinea Johnson

A Blessingway book

A portion of proceeds from the sale of this book will be donated to respite care for Alzheimer's caregiving.

Printed in the United States of America on 100% recycled paper in soy-based ink

Publisher's Cataloging-in-Publication Data

Ewing, Wayne, 1937–
    Tears in God's bottle: reflections on Alzheimer's
    caregiving / Wayne Ewing ; photographs by Dasha Wright
    Ewing ; with a foreword by Dorothy Ives. -- 1st ed.
    p. cm.
    LCCN: 98-75059
    ISBN: 0-9667547-0-0

    1. Caregivers--Religious life. 2. Alzheimer's disease--
Patients--Home care. 3. Caring--Religious aspects--
Christianity. 4. Ewing, Wayne. 1937–
5. Caregivers--Biography. I. Ewing, Dasha Wright.
II. Title.

BV4910.9.E95 1999   248.8'6
                       QB198-1537

10 9 8 7 6 5 4 3 2 1

Ann Margaret Wentz Ewing, PhD
(1935–1995)

ACKNOWLEDGMENTS

Remembering those who walked with me in the terror and joy of caregiving is an act of Eucharist: my sons, Christopher, Peter, Gregory; my daughters-in-law, Mary, Dasha; my granddaughter, Elizabeth; Ann's siblings, Tom, Alan, Rebecca, Sara, Gwen, and her late mother, Margaret Blessley Wentz; Fr. Bill Willson and the good people of St. Luke's Episcopal Mission, Westcliffe, Colorado, and all my colleagues at the *Wet Mountain Tribune;* the physicians and nurses who attended Ann, and especially the generous-hearted staff of Namasté Alzheimer Center, Colorado Springs; the countless friends who so awesomely gave of their time, energies, prayers, and presence, enveloping us in unimaginable compassion.

There was a second walk, that of my own recovery, as represented by the writing of these reflections. And so, too, there is a second act of Eucharist for those who nurtured me in this work: Myra, Tillie, Ruth, Jerry, Dawn, Lydia of the Alzheimer's Family Support Group in Española, New Mexico; the circle of readers who laughed and wept with me through the process, Dorothy, Steve and Jane, June, Carla and Tony—who opened their home to me as I first collected these meditations—and again, my sons and family. The words would not have found their way to the page without the support of Ellen Kleiner, my loving editor. Nor would the pages have found their shape without the creative hands and eyes of Dasha, Richard Harris, and Christinea Johnson.

For Wendy Caroll, the woman of valor and soul support in my life, these words from Torah, for her refining touch:

> Strength and dignity are her clothing,
> and she laughs at the time to come.
> She opens her mouth with wisdom,
> and the teaching of kindness is on her tongue . . .
> let her works bless her.
> —Proverbs 31:26, 31

My daughter-in-law, whose photographs grace this book, wishes to thank the following people:

Greg Ewing, for his love, patience, inspiration, and help in learning life's lessons; Sam and Brenda Wright, for their unwavering belief in me; Mary Margaret Frederick, for her faith, wisdom, and guidance; Carrington (Canny) Weems, for teaching me so much and for contributing his time and expertise to this project; Wayne Ewing, for giving me the opportunity to honor Ann in this way; Susan, Sally, Margaret, Beth, and Yael, for their support and encouragement.

CONTENTS

FOREWORD

There is a time, an eternal moment, when two souls are present in union with God. It is the time of transition when one is leaving the body and the other has yet to fulfill their earthly contract. For the one remaining, there is a fire within the heart that burns as heartache.

So it was for Wayne Ewing during the long illness and transition of his beloved wife, Ann. Most of us turn away from painful memories—not Wayne. In this poignant recall, *Tears in God's Bottle*, he shares in a most intimate and insightful way his last years with Ann, who was diagnosed at age fifty-five with Alzheimer's disease.

In the midst of despair moving across stormy seas of the unknown, Wayne brings us a genius of speaking to the heart of things as he paints a canvas of memory and images. We are taken with him on a journey—a holy calling of courage and self-sacrifice.

Wayne is an exquisite writer and a moving poet. Throughout his numerous traumatic experiences with pain and troubled thoughts, we catch the soul of a man who seems to have ascended into the divine universal flow. Negativity is stripped away while he grapples with the devilish aspects of the disease, and Wayne emerges triumphant.

There is a strong message here for those of us who have suffered the loss of a spouse or loved one. Even though we know our dear ones have returned to the heart of God, the agony of separation is immense. So it was with me when, after a long illness and several massive surgeries, my beloved Bard, Burl Ives, made his transition. Wayne's words create positive and healing energy around the wounds. The song of love changes in its frequency, and although the physical is no longer with us, the divine complement of our union lives on.

DOROTHY IVES
Anacortes, Washington

PROLOGUE

In the fall of her fifty-fifth year my beloved spouse, Ann, said to me, with a mixture of anger, humor, and candid stress, "I don't think I'm going to make it to the end of my life." Her premonition could not have been more accurate. The following June Ann was diagnosed with early-onset Alzheimer's disease, and after three years of at-home care, at the age of fifty-eight, she became a resident at Namasté Alzheimer Center in Colorado Springs.

Alzheimer's disease, thief of time and personality, abducted Ann from the full journey of her life. Each of us Alzheimer's caregivers has experienced this slow but steady diminishment of a loved one; they leave us prematurely, often in the fullness of life, while we remain by their side.

I had been by Ann's side most of my life. We met in the ninth grade at Mechanicsburg High School, where we would go each weekday from our outlying Pennsylvania homes. Ann, the oldest of six children, lived with her family on a lovely farm; I was an only child who lived with working parents in the village of Shiremanstown. Ann initiated our first date with an invitation to the Sadie Hawkins' Day Dance in the school gym. Off we went—me a shy Li'l Abner and Ann a feisty Sadie Hawkins.

We married a year after graduating from Pennsylvania colleges thirty miles apart, I from Gettysburg and Ann from Wilson, and nurtured each other through doctoral programs, mine in theological studies and Ann's in women's issues and feminist therapy. In the late 1960s, after birthing three sons, we moved our young family to Singapore for five years. There I taught theology at Trinity Theological College, and Ann cofounded and operated a day-care program for adults newly discharged from mental health facilities. Returning to the United States in 1971, we became leaders in the gender equality movement, helped establish a free school for adolescents, practiced together as psychotherapists, and became great friends.

Ann went on to become a well-known feminist therapist in Denver, the culmination of a professional life built with wit, wisdom, joy, and commitment to health and wholeness. Although small in stature, she was seen as expansive in soul—one of life's lovers and cocreators.

The diagnosis of Alzheimer's disease came as a double jolt. Not only did I see the illness threatening Ann's exquisite well-being but also a major part of my own life was about to be ripped away. Soon Ann, lost in space and time, was both gone and still there; was well yet very ill; saw yet had no vision; heard yet had little understanding. I was terrified about being too ill-equipped as a caregiver to cope lovingly with such a hideously debiliting illness.

Alzheimer's disease was originally described in 1906 by the Swiss physician Alois Alzheimer. He had carefully charted the degeneration of a patient whose profile was uncannily like Ann's—a bright, engaged woman in her early fifties. The cause of such degeneration, unknown to him, remained unknown at the time of Ann's illness. Medical science was beginning to progress, however, from simply observing and managing the affliction to discovering and prescribing medications that slowed its advance *in some people*. I collaborated with medical research and medication trials with a curious combination of hope and despair, but pursuing a variety of medical advances did not help me cope as a caregiver.

Grappling with the fallout left week by week in the wake of this illness was equally ill-fated, for Alzheimer's savage attacks seemed to threaten the very soul of my loved one. As Charlie, a dear friend, said to me toward the end of Ann's time at home, "It's not like cancer of the belly or the bone, where you have something to fight and someone to fight it with; Alzheimer's is a *disease of the soul*." For a time it seemed that Charlie was right.

Behaviorally, cognitively, and spiritually, Alzheimer's does attack those faculties traditionally associated with the soul: memory, knowledge, and intention. So when the memory, thoughts, and will of our loved ones disappear before our eyes, it is as if their soul were under siege. Moreover, the soul is conceived of as the place where human beings touch the infinite; graced with a sense of past, present, and future, the soul anticipates eternity. Thus when our loved ones' minds go awry with Alzheimer's dementia, it seems that the soul is in some way ill. After entertaining such perceptions, I began to appreciate how the soul is *so much more* than the body housing it, and decided to no longer think of the human soul in the limited terms of disease.

Defying this deadly disease through either research or denial was not helping me remain attentive to the minute-to-minute struggles of caregiving. On the contrary, accumulating information and listening to my internal voice of resistance often distracted me from the task at hand. Then a curious dynamic came to my attention: I noticed that as Ann diminished, I increased. Little by little, I was becoming for her a source of memory, a problem solver, a decision maker, a compass, and clock. And, as in the tradition of the Jewish Sabbath, I was experiencing an enhancement of soul each time the activities of my loved one's soul were added to my own.

Yes, I realized, resources *are* available to me as a caregiver. What I needed to learn to trust was not necessarily new scientific information or contemporary interpretations of illness, but rather a very *old* knowledge—a soul knowledge. Soon afterward I immersed myself in the realm of biblically informed spirituality. Even though formal theology, in which I had been well-schooled, was not of much help, the wisdom of the Bible, on which that theology was based, opened a door to unexpected spiritual growth. At the time of Ann's diagnosis I was a deacon in the Episcopal church, and during her illness I was ordained a priest. Although I have since resigned my offices in the church, the daily practice of prayer and scripture reading helped me assuage my fears and become more present and supportive in my round-the-clock ministrations with Ann.

Faith grows in the besieged environment of caregiving. For me, daily Bible readings fostered wondrous growth, all the while easing wrenching situations, putting me in touch with the mystery of creation, and joining my tears with those of others who were conversing with God. I could not understand this horrid disease, but I *could* begin to use the power of the soul and devote myself to expanding that energy. I could also accept the invitation that had come wrapped in the trappings of Alzheimer's caregiving—namely, to enter anew the family of God and be made whole once again.

Oddly, our culture mistakes curing for healing, and our religious traditions confuse perfection with wholeness. The measure of human beings, Ann used to say, is not perfection, but fullness and wholeness; perfection is a measure of *objects*, for which we have a federal Bureau of Standards overseen by the Department of Commerce. "Stop trying to be perfect," she would chide, "and just try being whole." Wholeness, for her, was the behavioral and spiritual measure of a human life lived well.

Ann also believed that the passage from St. Matthew that reads, "Be perfect, therefore, as your heavenly father is perfect" (5:48), is a puritanically mischievous translation designed to promote guilt and hopelessness among God's creatures. "Read instead," Ann insisted, "'Be whole, therefore, and full, as is God.'" The Greek word *teleios*, which can be translated as either "whole" or "perfect," supports Ann's own mischief with the text.

My search for healing and wholeness during the march of Alzheimer's disease is perhaps best reflected in a letter I sent to people around the world who had become woven into our tapestry of life. The words came naturally one tormented evening in the depths of Ann's last, failing winter at home. Sitting by our bed, where she appeared to be seeking in sleep the peace she had not found while awake, I wrote:

Dear Friends,

I trust you know that had I the time and energy, I would be writing you individually and at length. That is not to be, and I am sorry for it.

I am writing because I want you to know that we are losing Ann to the mists of Alzheimer's disease. After fending off demands of the savage disease for over two and a half years since its diagnosis, Ann is slipping away. As our neurologist put it to us last week, "Ann's reserve tanks are depleted." It's not that the disease is speeding up physiologically; it's simply that the plaque is spreading to places where Ann had had her compensatory powers, and she has them no more. We are doing all the right things and yet losing ground almost daily. I do not think we will make it to the end of the year with our at-home care resources.

Friends in our small Colorado community are awesomely caring and supportive, bringing meals twice a week and spelling me for a few hours by sitting or walking with Ann. We use Custer County's home health-care program and will soon begin day care in Pueblo as well.

Refuse to believe that victims of Alzheimer's disease do not suffer; Ann suffers. She who in her friendships, parenting, and professional life always freed others from victimization is now, heinously, a victim. I weep for this hateful thing that is happening to her.

What I ask of you, while there is still a moment, is a photo or a note that Ann might take with her into her terror, and that I might use to tell her a tale or two more in our painful, loving walk into the fog.

One power that Ann still exercises is her capacity for praise, love, and blessing. In our sorrow we send these to you and relish the gift you have been to her powerful life.

> *Peace,*
>
> *Wayne*

In response to this letter emerging from the dark night of my soul, there came an infusion of spiritual energy in the form of cards, phone calls, letters, and photographs. Those healing salves carried me through and beyond caregiving. They showed me that at the heart of life, beyond quarks and chaos and hyperspace, there lies an unspeakable beauty; a glorious covenant between the Creator and the order and disorder of creation; an enchanting, peaceful bond of love with all that threatens love; and a striking rainbow cast against the thundering gray heavens.

The collection of writings that follows addresses many of the spiritual challenges I encountered in my walk with

Ann. Each one opens with a biblical quotation followed by an illness-related dilemma, my response to it, and how the opening verse helped me interpret my experience. Each reflection closes with a prayer that I invite you to hold in your heart during a quiet moment set apart from your caregiving.

These reflections celebrate the strength of the soul, the power God gives to the helpless, and the offer of divine sanctuary as we wend our way with a loved one down the unknown and often dreadful byways of Alzheimer's disease. They also honor a commitment Ann and I made soon after her diagnosis—to live each day in joy and fullness. I hope you will find these passages helpful and healing on your caregiving walk. As you read them, either in sequence or in any order you choose, know in your heart that to draw on the resources of soul when the mind and body fail is to be received into the holy and to be at home in God.

When everything around you shatters and breaks, never again to come together in the same way, may you find restoration and peace. While illness steals away, in bits and pieces, the gentle fabric of your life, may you and your loved one embark on a spiritually rich journey to wholeness.

ON PAIN AND LOSS

1

OUR TEARS IN GOD'S BOTTLE

When I am afraid, I put my trust in you. In God, whose word
I praise, in God I trust; I am not afraid. You have kept count
of my tossings; put my tears in your bottle.

Psalm 56:3, 4, 8

I admitted Ann to Namasté Alzheimer Center on the
Wednesday prior to Palm Sunday. The busyness, and business,
of admitting her occupied my every thought for the rest of the
week. While weary, I was not left alone to cope with the painful
demands of this time, for my son and daughter-in-law had welcomed me into their nearby home for several days. Their quiet,
unassuming acceptance of my pain, congruent with their own,
shepherded me through this very difficult transition.

I returned home in time for the somber yet festive Eucharist
of Palm Sunday. That Holy Week, thank God, was filled with
study and devotion in the small Episcopal mission where I
served as one of two priests. Every evening I was prayerfully

engaged with the congregation, and I haltingly began to learn the rhythms of visiting with Ann at Namasté while moving on without her by my side. At last the Feast of the Resurrection arrived, and with great joy the assembled worshipers joined in affirming one of the most ancient refrains of Christian liturgy: "Christ is risen! Christ is risen indeed, Alleluia!"

It fell to me that Easter to proclaim God's word in the homily of the Eucharist. The message I brought seemed uncomplicated and sure. In my grief and turmoil, I spoke of the solace of the restoration awaiting us all in Christ's victory over death. This was truly an "Alleluia!" brightening my twisted, tormented days.

During my drive back from church to our lovely secluded home in a ponderosa forest overlooking the Wet Mountain Valley and the east face of the Sangre de Cristo range of the Rocky Mountains, I shattered. By the time I was into the Wet Mountains, I had to pull over to the side of the isolated gravel road and weep fiercely for a long, painful time. Mourning had suddenly overtaken me, and I felt broken and wasted.

Certainly, I had cried before. In fact, tears had been fairly constant companions during the journey from diagnosis through caretaking to full-time residential nursing-home care. But these tears burned with a bitterness I had not felt before, washing my face in a strange, harsh warmth.

It seemed that I was at last catching up with my grief. In my determination to meet Ann's needs, I had been too busy, too exhausted, and too intent on preparing for the next wounded moment to mourn. So it was not surprising that I now met myself in great sadness.

As I eventually pulled back onto the road and began the last climb up the steep winding hill to our home, the words of Psalm 56 came to me. This psalm had been part of my readings during Lent, and I had noted it as a timely reference to the depth of my sorrow and to the solace all grieving souls might find in God's presence.

In God's bottle, I concluded, my tears had indeed been stored. I recalled that tears were once so precious they were retained in tiny vials made especially for them so that people could revere them at will. Alas, because human beings long ago abandoned the practice, there are no more vials for our tears—except for God's bottle.

Now I realized God had chosen that moment on the Feast of the Resurrection to empty the bottle of my tears. It was apparent that there is a consecrated, holy place where our tears are devoutly collected, and there comes a moment when in an offertory of immense grief, the bottle is broken and our tears are returned to us. It is a moment of wonder and grace.

I thanked God for endowing me with tears, and for keeping these tears in a bottle until that holy time when they were spilled on my face, my heart, my love, and my memory with care and reverence.

❧

O God, whose invisible hands hold my visible sadness, catch up my tears that I may finally weep with You, and You with me, one in sorrow, and then in joy. Amen.

2

GOD'S SELFISH TEARS

As Jesus came near and saw the city, he wept over it, saying,
"If you, even you, had only recognized on this day the things
that make for peace!"

St. Luke 19:41, 42

My crying was so profuse after Ann's admission to
Namasté that I soon developed an ability to distinguish the
different types of tears I shed. As they became more familiar
to me, I began to name them.

I also started seeing a therapist once a week, for I had recognized a need to be with my mourning in a safe and intimate
setting. Bonnie, who was no stranger to grieving, helped me
prevent my profound sadness from slipping into debilitating
depression.

One day I told Bonnie that I had identified three different
types of tears. First, I explained, there are "sorrow tears" that

come with feelings of deep, stark sorrow for Ann. Seeing her cut off in such a heinous manner from the fullness of her life moved me to cries of anguish for this woman who had once been so competent, bright, and present to others. A feminist therapist who was sought out for her sensitivity to the agonies of oppression, she was also a loving and supportive mother, mother-in-law, and grandmother, and was just coming into the years of blessing that a grown family can bestow. She was preparing to blossom again in the years ahead of her, but time came to an end before her living did. About a year after her diagnosis, Ann had written a note to herself that read in part, "I feel cheated, cheated, cheated!" I wept for her great pain.

I also shed "loss tears," I told Bonnie, that come as I mourn the loss of my companionship with Ann and our visions of partnering into the future. Time ended for our relationship with each other and shifted to an extraordinary relationship with the disease itself, which was nothing like the plans we had so cherished. Where we had foreseen traveling and offering services to new communities, there was instead progressive anxiety and fear. Where we had envisioned joy and comfort in each other's company, there was now torment and uncertainty.

The third type of tears I described to Bonnie were "selfish tears" I was not proud of. I told her how I cried sometimes for myself, for the way in which my world had turned so unexpectedly from multidimensional living to the more narrow focus of daily caregiving. I confided to her how I mourned the separation from my hopes, dreams, and desires for an ordinary life.

"Why *wouldn't* you mourn your personal loss?" Bonnie

asked in a soft voice. "You, too, have been assaulted by this disease, and you may have borne even more of its devastation than Ann during her passage into the unknown. Why do you call such mourning selfish?"

My mind filled with answers: Because caregivers are supposed to give selflessly and not count their losses. Because caregivers should remain strong and confident, and not give in to self-pity. Because caregivers need to be tough and avoid displays of weakness. The more answers I came up with, the more shame I felt in crying for myself.

Then I remembered Jesus' tears and great sorrow, a sadness unto death, while in prayer at Gethsemane a few hours before his crucifixion. Surely, I thought, these tears, God's tears, were being shed in response to an imminent loss of community and the impending separation from devotion, ministry, and love.

Over the city of Jerusalem Jesus also wept for himself, a rabbi forsaken by his followers: "How often have I desired to gather your children, as a hen gathers her brood under her wings, and you were not willing!" (St. Luke 13:34). I realized that longing is within God, too, and hopes that are dashed for God become the source of tears for the divine self. Moreover, in the Garden of Gethsemane, Jesus' acceptance of the next hours of his life came by way of mourning: through remembrance of the past, recognition of the severed present, and sheer anguish over the imploding terror before him.

Tears for one's self, I concluded, needn't be construed as selfish, but instead deserve to be honored. These are "truth tears" that express the pain of spirit bowed before loss, separation, and death. No longer do I fault myself for crying over my losses. Instead, I now weep in the truth, and God weeps with me.

∽

O God, who weeps in the truth and pain of separation and loss, may You find my tears equally holy, and so lift me into Your heart. Amen.

3

DIVINE JEALOUSY

For I am going to die in this land without crossing over the
Jordan, but you are going to cross over to take possession of
that good land. So be careful not to forget the covenant that
God made with you, and not to make for yourselves an idol
in the form of anything that God has forbidden you. For God
is a devouring fire, a jealous God.

Deuteronomy 4:22–24

As Ann's capacities diminished, I often carried a hardened,
cold heart while looking at romancing couples, joyful lovers,
hand-in-hand eye-locked partners. Wherever I saw them,
whether in a mall, after church services, on a forest path, on
a bustling street, or in a quiet restaurant, I felt anger in their
presence. I rarely knew, of course, if they were really in love,
but nonetheless upon seeing them, I felt tumultuous pain in
my heart, and the chill of a maddening hate.

Psychologically, I knew what was happening. Deprived of

the long love of my life, I was in deep mourning for love. Having seen the living soul of my beloved ripped away while her face, limbs, and voice were still before me, I was aching profoundly for the fresh bloom of love. What had happened to the laughing Ann who would say to me, "Yeah, I love you, but sometimes I don't *like* you"? Where had the Ann gone who would spontaneously call me at my office and invite me to drop everything to meet her in City Park for a gourmet picnic? Seeing my love wither, I compensated by becoming bitter whenever my eye fell on what looked like loving couples.

Even though I understood the psychology behind my feelings, I didn't apprehend what was going on in my soul. Only when I realized that I was constantly falling back on the cynicism of Ecclesiastes' "Vanity of vanities! All is vanity" (1:2) did I begin to see that I had turned the integrity of my love for Ann into a hatred of loving. Listening to Spirit, I discovered the holy rage and righteous anger that come when love is twisted and broken by illness.

Yes, I decided, I am going to die in this land without the fullness of my love with Ann, separated from the love that was eternally fresh between us. I am going to die on this side of the Jordan, against the mouth of Sheol, bereft of the wholeness of my life, while others cross over into that rich land of love and comfort.

Never before had I grasped the intense jealousy of God. Surely I knew that God's name is "The Jealous One" (Exodus 34:14), and that both the Mosaic and Deuteronomic renderings of the Ten Commandments define God's life as jealous.

But I had attributed this interpretation of God's self-disclosure to the "old" covenant between God and God's people. As I saw it, the archaic wrath, vengefulness, and destruction had been "redone" in the so-called "new" covenant.

Eventually, a shift in perspective allowed me to see how shortsighted I had been, even while living within reach of God's continuing jealousy. How refreshed I felt as my denial was washed away and I awakened to a divine jealousy forged of boundless love! With that I was able to cast off my dishonoring bitterness and truly embrace my love of Ann.

As she slipped away into lost places, of course I missed loving her in the old familiar ways. It had been so easy between us to be close, to slide away from work and worry into a comfortable cocoon of affection. Yet I was no longer enveloped in self-pitying envy. I was able to shed my former readiness to negate other lovers' paths to joy.

I now know that being awakened to the sacredness of jealousy, being led to the ache for wholeness borne in the experience of love, has come to me from the heart of love. Today, I look anew at enraptured faces, young and old, intense in passion and soft in laughter, as the promise of that good and rich land beyond the Jordan. My wishes for these people are unceasing: O that you might walk there with the joy Ann and I embraced! O that you might taste of the honey and fat there, drink the wine of its fruits, and live together to bless its Creator!

Now when loving couples cross my path, I am no longer envious, but sacredly jealous. And I am learning how St. Paul came to say to his beloved Corinthians, "I feel a divine jealousy for you" (II Corinthians 11:2). To such enraptured people I silently say: The jealousy I feel for you who seem to be in love while on your short, sweet walk through life is God's own jealousy. The jealous wish I have for you is that you come to know and bless God; that you rejoice in being gifted in that good and rich land with this most precious connection between you and your beloved; and that you live with these gifts faithfully and well, nobly and in holiness. For this is the pathway of God's walk with us.

❧

O God, whose pathway is love, so lead me to cherish love in my midst that I may be jealous of Your love and, by Your doing, jealous of my love. Amen.

4

SEPARATION AND UNION

Meanwhile, standing near the cross of Jesus were his mother, and his mother's sister, Mary the wife of Clopas, and Mary Magdalene. When Jesus saw his mother and the disciple whom he loved [St. John] standing beside her, he said to his mother, "Woman, here is your son." Then he said to the disciple, "Here is your mother." And from that hour the disciple took her into his own house.

St. John 19:25b–27

Some days I had no thought or desire beyond the need at hand: a meal, a bath, a walk, reading aloud. In the grip of such immediacy, I would often feel my aching loss of Ann to this cruel dementia. And then I would marvel at the interplay between pain and compassion. I would sense how pain and compassion, loss and love, engaged in a strangely spiraling dance, whirling slowly into a night that was never dark, a void that was never empty, a mystery that was not at all puzzling.

I would dwell on Mary, mother of Jesus, whose inner

strength carried her through profound pain and loss. Sons had come miraculously to many biblical women: Sarah, the mother of Isaac; Rebekah, the mother of Esau and Jacob; Rachel, the mother of Joseph and Benjamin; the unnamed mother of Samson; Hannah, the mother of Samuel; and Elizabeth, the mother of John the Baptist. But Mary alone lived in the shadow of a child's death.

What, I wondered, might have been going on in Mary's heart at the foot of the cross bearing the body of her loved one? It seemed like a strange intertwining of separation and union created by pain and loss. I believed that what I saw in this brief account of St. John was the give and take of care in the midst of love. Mary's pain had become the occasion for Jesus' compassion, while her compassion had been instanced by Jesus' pain.

Compassion did not ease the pain for either the mother or the son. The son would die; the mother was in terror of death, and would mourn. In fact, compassion and tenderness, expressed in touching and kind words, heightened pain. Pain fed compassion; compassion fed pain.

This was also the dance *I* was dancing. Even though my body ached for it, my mind envisioned it, and my soul prayed for it, not for a minute would I have abandoned the cross of my loved one's dying. I stood, like Mary before me, in silence, pain, and confusion. And though surrounded by others, like her I was alone, I had done the utmost I was capable of in nurturing, caring, and being present—and yet it had not been enough to stanch the flow of pain.

But despite the confusion, there were wondrous times when Ann smiled, spoke, flashed with quickened recognition and love. These were moving moments, like Jesus enfolding his mother with care from his broken dying: "Woman, here is your son." When Ann suddenly brightened with laughter and sparkling eyes, and *saw* me, I was once again enfolded into her love. It was a glorious sensation, even though this exchange of care and love heightened pain.

Although Mary experienced again her son's supreme love in the tender gift of his beloved friend's home, the flow of life returned to loss and pain. Yet now pain was lifted to a new place, a place that was different from yesterday. It became a pain for tomorrow that carried today's gift.

Perhaps the only thing that stood between me and bitterness or deadly despair was this delicate breath of my spouse's love, at times so evident. This seemingly fragile affection gradually formed a solid rock wall that kept me on this side of the dark in the light, this side of the void in fullness, within the mystery of the known.

❧

O God, who turns the face of pain into the face of love, may I allow myself to be seen in love, and begin to walk again in light. Amen.

5

LOVE'S FIRE

For love is strong as death, passion fierce as the grave. Its flashes are flashes of fire, a raging flame. Many waters cannot quench love, neither can floods drown it.

Song of Solomon 8:6, 7

At times I suspected that the fire of love was in danger of being quenched by the floodwaters of Alzheimer's disease. Amid the daily moment-to-moment demands of seeing to Ann's needs, and of assisting her with orientation, there seemed to be neither time nor space for love.

How false a conjecture this turned out to be, how errant the musings of a weary caregiver! Consistently, out of Ann's torment and confusion, she would call out to me, "I love you. I love you." Until the day she lost the ability to speak, any time the fleeting recognition of a caregiver came storming through the fog of her disease, she would grasp the person's arm and whisper these words.

It is not for me to say what Ann meant by "love" in the ragged states of her mind and heart, for meaning is not what she focused on in such tender moments. What matters is that the savage disease did not wrench *the presence* of love from her heart or her soul. Ann's love, flaring out from the depths of her soul, sealed upon the moment, like a flame of God, a lightning-quick truth about her lost place, revealing the part of her that grasped the one thing that matters about love—its simple *existence*.

Love, I came to realize, is as strong as death, and wrestling with Alzheimer's slow dying uses an energy death cannot comprehend. Death as the partner of evil has never fathomed the quality God bestowed upon love—that of gift. For to love, to be loved, and to be love in service to another are all holy gifts. So when my knees buckled in exhaustion, my mind reeled for a creative insight, and my heart ached for the easy relationship Ann and I had once enjoyed, my soul was nourished by the strength love brought to death's slow march.

As I continued to experience Ann's love in the midst of her suffering, I came to relish this surge of the holy at the lip of the grave. All along the way, step by faltering step, in pauses by the streamside of life, love challenged death. Here there was to be no simple victory for death. I saw that the fire of Sheol—the place of death—dims before the purifying, cleansing flame of God that is fueled by love.

As time passed, I learned to raise my sights above my diminishing energies. By grace, I was able to look beyond the ashen glow of Sheol to the flame of love as it flashed through

Ann's expressions of love. God was not going to let us, weak as we were, overwhelmed by the demands of this disease as we were, go down to death without love. Now I am beginning to believe that no flood can quench the fiery gift of love felt in the white heat of living in the presence of God.

∾

O God, whose raging flame of love casts a light into all my darkness, quicken my soul to live within Your fire with grace and ease. Amen.

6

EVIL UNDONE

But if it is by the finger of God that I cast out the demons,
then the kingdom of God has come to you.

St. Luke 11:20

One day when Ann ran terrified from the kitchen as the tele-
phone rang, I became convinced that this thieving disease was
"evil," even though I knew it was customary to ascribe evil only
to moral agents. At first, I thought it inappropriate to claim that
the bizarre plaque that infects brain tissue in Alzheimer's
patients is evil. Yet ultimately I could find no better way to
regard this horror. The term stuck regardless of the questions I
asked myself: Am I simply to think it quaint and medically
naive that scripture repeatedly alludes to the evil at work in disease? Am I to shrug off all notions of evil at the heart of illness
because of the presumed amoral consequences of disease?

Despite my conclusion, I could not bring myself to regard

the sway of evil I was witnessing as something personified by Satan. Nor did it have anything to do with the evil of judgment, or with some point on a scale of immorality.

I then realized how easy it would have been to dismiss the spiritual weight of evil in the context of disease. Because so much in our world is called "evil"—prejudice, greed, injustice, rapaciousness, apathy, those who disagree with us—it would be possible to conclude that hardly anything is evil since we would have nothing left to contrast it to. And yet I remained certain that evil was more than a flip word for what troubles me.

The plain and simple truth was that Ann's battle with Alzheimer's disease had transported me beyond all theological and sociological barriers to a face-to-face encounter with evil. The invasion of her being had become a vast larceny of personality. A daughter of God was being mercilessly trampled into the merest remnant of her humanity.

In a moment filled with grace, I learned I was not alone in viewing this situation as evil. Ann had been given a secondary diagnosis of progressive supranuclear palsy (PSP), a neurological disorder of unknown origin causing tremors that randomly racked her hands, arms, feet, legs, and head. When she was deep into her diminishment and speaking indistinctly or in one-word "sentences," Ann told a son and daughter-in-law who were spoon-feeding her a pureed supper, "I can't help this." A blast of recognition had broken through Ann's loss of volition. And in that spirited moment, she had acknowledged that her affliction was evil—a power beyond her will, leading her into a place where she had not chosen to be.

Neither the finger of God nor a medical breakthrough had lessened the force of this evil. Indeed, it had been so pervasive that the assault of the disease quickly became an assault on my own faith. I began to wonder, is there a power working against life that defies not only science but also God?

Jesus' astute rabbinical argument, quoted above from St. Luke, gave me some solace. I found comfort in this reminder that ultimately evil is within God's reach. And I felt consoled when I recalled that the healing narratives of the New Testament, filled as they are with images of powers struggling with one another for supremacy, repeatedly convey the victory of light over darkness, of love and compassion over fear, pain, and evil.

One such passage focuses on the reversal of bad fortune: "Go and tell John what you have seen and heard: the blind receive their sight, the lame walk, the lepers are cleansed, the deaf hear, the dead are raised, the poor have good news brought to them" (St. Luke 7:22). Although I could not report, as these messengers did so long ago, that a loved one was restored, I began to see that these demons of affliction were indeed repelled by love.

Ultimately, I realized that in the face of Alzheimer's disease, care is the finger of God. The mere extension of kindness—a smile, a hug, a kiss, brushing my loved one's hair, feeding her, dressing her, applying makeup to her, or singing a song—invited God to reach into an evil I myself could not penetrate.

As a result, I now know that evil cringes in the presence of such focused, attentive love. Affection, although incapable of curing the disease, heals the wounds of the person assaulted, for affection is the finger of God.

❧

O God, whose finger turns every evil into its undoing, lead me by Your healing hand into that good place where comfort and vision and peace prevail. Amen.

7

REGIONS DARK AND DEEP

Are your wonders known in the darkness, or your saving help in the land of forgetfulness? Why do you cast me off? Why do you hide your face from me? I suffer your terrors; I am desperate.

Psalm 88:12–15

Some of my darkest moments as a caregiver were when, in Ann's presence, my aloneness was all I could experience. At such times I would think that there was no one in the room but me, no reality other than this loss, nowhere to be standing but in this terrifying and lonely landscape. My only solace came while feeling the pulse of despair within scripture. In the lament of Psalm 88, for example, not even a glimmer of hope appears; reading it aloud, I was able to hear that darkness is *all* there is. This loss, I told myself, is like being slain, for it has deadened me with sorrow.

From this land of living death I could see "the land of forgetfulness" where Ann paced, measuring its contours. This was a place where the usual marks of orientation and identity had disappeared into homelessness and silence; where signatures of the familiar had been blown away like sand in the desert; where vision had been met with confusion, sound with anxiety, touch with fear.

Psalm 88 poses a frightening question that remains unanswered: *Is God's help known in the land of forgetfulness?* The impression is that Sheol is beyond God's reach. As Isaiah put it, "Those who go down to the Pit cannot hope for God's fruitfulness" (38:18). But, I wondered, can there actually be such a place where I am cast off, God's face is hidden, and the last word really is, "I suffer your terrors; I am desperate"?

I discovered the answer was yes; and in the unending darkness I experienced due to Ann's dementia, I thanked God for the psalmist's profound integrity in despair and pain. In Psalm 88 the crushing power of illness, loneliness, and hopelessness stands stark and bold. Even the silhouette of pain becomes lost in the overwhelming darkness of the psalmist's reality. By contrast, Lamentations—the psaltery of sorrow over the Babylonian destruction of Jerusalem—lifts up hope for eventual deliverance and celebrates the constancy of God's love. Even Job countenances the final peace of God settling over excruciating pain and loss.

And yet the lament over darkness expressed in Psalm 88 is not thrown into the darkness, but is given to God, for the psalm has been lifted up to God. Its tone, although desperate, is in song to God: "When, at night, I cry out in your presence, let my prayer come before you, incline your ear to my cry" (1, 2).

In time, my pain, as well, was given to God. As the light of this message shone on my darkness of soul, I discovered I was being asked to be real with myself, to be honest with my pain over loss and separation, and to lay out even my most terrifying moments before God's great passion. Now, alone no longer, I welcome the company of the psalmist, who laments with me.

∽

O God, who welcomes and waits for my cry from the farthest reaches of my despair, help me always to be in truth with You and myself, and with my pain and loss. Amen.

ON PRAYER

8

PRAYER AND WILL

And this is the boldness we have in God, that if we ask anything according to God's will, God hears us. And if we know
that God hears us in whatever we ask, we know that we have
obtained the requests made of God.

I John 5:14, 15

Every prayer I lifted to God in the advanced stages of Ann's
disease was answered with affirmation and love. But I had to
learn the difference between prayers and wishes, fantasies,
hopes, or dreams.

When I wished that the disease would go away, my wishes were shattered. But when I prayed to wake up the next day
with sufficient strength to meet Ann's needs, my prayers were
answered.

When I fantasized that Ann would return and "be herself," my fantasies were dashed to pieces against the rocky
realities of the disease. But when I prayed that during the

coming day Ann would be cared for and loved, my prayers were answered.

When I hoped that a wonder drug would be discovered to cure Alzheimer's disease, my hopes were confounded. But when I prayed that Ann and I could be replenished through the nurturance of those who loved us, my prayers were answered.

When I dreamed about a reversal of the relentless march of the disease, my dreams became nightmares. But when I prayed that I might continue to be part of Ann's security and comfort for one more day, my prayers were answered.

Adhering to prayer rather than escaping through wishes, fantasies, hopes, or dreams was painful and frightening. However, I soon learned that I was not glorifying God with my aversion to the truth. And as time went by, praying and devotion came more naturally.

At first it had been difficult to empty my soul to God with phrases like, "Yet not what I want, but what You want." Similarly, I had locked out from my prayers the power of "Your will be done." Why? Because to have lived as if a will beyond my own were active in my life would have been to harbor gnawing, disempowering questions about self, control, authority, and decision making.

Then, too, I wanted somehow to protect God, or at least my image of God. I imagined that if I put God's will at the heart of my personal life, then God would have a lot of responsibility for a variety of ungodly matters. And if I saw God in connection with the world's overwhelming sorrow and evil, God's image would become tainted and God's glory dissipated.

But God's grace upended my foolishness. I soon realized that it was enough to take care of myself and do what I could to care for Ann, that I didn't need to take care of God too! Besides, God could care for both of us much better than I.

Gradually, I came to see that when I relinquished my will and asked God's will to enter my life, prayer took on a new dynamic. I realized that prayer is not about wishing, fantasizing, hoping, or dreaming but about releasing desires and concerns to the heart of God. Thus I began putting into words my reality not as I hoped it might be but as it *was*. My praying became bold enough to ask for the aid of divine will, and humble enough to meet the lover of souls—the Holy One, God.

∾

O God, who beckons me to prayer that I might hear You, open my heart until my prayer becomes You, and You become my prayer. Amen.

9

BEING PRAYED FOR

Rejoice in hope, be patient in suffering, persevere in prayer.

Romans 12:12

Scores of friends persevered in prayer for Ann and me. We knew we were prayed for unceasingly and that this prayer originated in areas all around the globe, so that we were being lifted into God's heart every hour. Knowing that we were so regularly knitted into prayer awakened a new eucharistic awareness.

I was already familiar with offering focused prayers, but I began to learn more about living as the object of other people's recurrent prayers. As the focus of our friends' daily prayers, I developed a keen sense of what a blessing it was to be moved into God's heart. Over time, living in rhythm with prayers on my behalf became as much a spiritual discipline as my own devotion to prayer.

New sensations began to arise within me. For example, I felt my soul—always alive and dancing with creation—being breathed upon by God. Also, I sensed that God blessed and molded my body. The surge of God's creation seemed to permeate my every thought and creative act, and in prayer I found the trace of God's holy breath. With an almost tactile sense, I could feel my soul begin a feathery glide into the heart of God.

Engaged with the petitions directed to God for my sake, I experienced the presence of a sensate, soulful companion to my pain. In the creases of the night when my fractured sleep bolted me into wakefulness, and in the folds of the day as my bones ached with exhaustion, I could feel the "touch" of the caring suffering of God rise up from deep within my body.

Sometimes this sensation of being bound over into God's care seemed suffused with light, as if a glow were outlining all the dark edges of my life. With awe, I wondered what sense could detect light in the midst of this ugly dark disease? I believed that these beams of light penetrating my weariness were surely radiated by God's Holy Spirit while channeling the devout prayers of our friends into my otherwise darkened world. With each beam, I could absorb our friends' intentions for God to give me solace to ease Ann's suffering.

All these sensations came unbidden, with a racing heart accompanied sometimes by tears, other times by a smile. It was as if something in me were listening despite my preoccupation with Ann's needs.

Before long, I discovered that something inside me *was* listening: my soul, touched by God, was hearing the whispered prayers from friends around the world. And each time God breathed on me, I was quietly being invited to accept God's peace.

Although this gift borne on the bright wings of God did not cure Ann's disease, it helped heal me, restoring wholeness to the fractured existence that threatened to undo me and to unravel my love. As a result, I came to know the great peace that is transmitted by way of others' prayers. God's passion becomes entwined in the breath and rhythms of prayer, and even when the soul is distressed by disease, as Ann's was, serenity enters and peace suffuses the caring environment. We need only listen for the touch of friends' prayers.

❧

O God, who invites me to pray unceasingly for those who suffer, may I be led to hear the prayers lifted up for my sake, and so live within Your heart. Amen.

10

GIVING THANKS

From God's fullness we have all received, grace upon grace.

St. John 1:16

Early in my caregiving I was graced by Ann's joyous participation in the fullness of God's creation. Still living at home, she had not yet become uncommunicative. To the contrary, in the full bloom of that Rocky Mountain summer, she began to articulate the sense of beauty she perceived all around her.

Every morning and evening we would walk, rarely deviating from a one-mile path circling through the ponderosa forest around our home. We set no time limit for these excursions; in pleasant weather and with sufficient daylight remaining, we hiked for as long as we wished. As the summer unfolded, Ann increasingly slowed her pace, not from any physical disability, but because of a growing desire to see, smell, touch, and address each sweet moment of her experience.

She would kneel to caress a miniature cinquefoil peeking from a rock crevice, or to touch a budding button cactus, or to feel the freshness of moss and the rough texture of lichen. Occasionally, she paused to pick up a small piece of white quartz, holding it up to the sunlight, amazed by the translucence of solid rock. She pushed her head into piñon branches to smell sap and cones, and propped up seedling ponderosas with sticks and stones, scattering animal droppings around them for nourishment.

Often, Ann stopped in her tracks and lifted her head, listening to the rustle of aspen in the breeze, tracking the flight of birds, or following the retreating thump of deer spooked by our sudden presence. Those that did not run off would stay frozen, eye to eye with her as she spoke to them, saying, "Oh, it's so fine to see you today! Please stay with me!"

With awe, Ann absorbed both the large and the small aspects of nature. She would scan the hundred-mile range of the Sangre de Cristos to the west, marveling at the peaks, snowfields, and alpine vegetation. Then she would hunker down on the ground to observe a tiny spider webbing a home beneath a stone. After lying on her back, tracing the towering cumulus clouds rumbling up over the mountains, she would then roll onto her belly to watch a beetle scrambling through grasses and pine needles. "Look at the color of this petal," she would repeat several times as she touched a flower over and over again. And I would feel gifted to be with her in such peace and serenity when everything else in our world was crumbling away.

Ann was gathering up the glory of nature and seemed to cherish each of these events as if creation itself were greeting her with its beauty. What I so relished about these precious times was the way she celebrated their newness. Again and again she would say, "Do you see? Do you see? It's so lovely, so lovely." What might have been considered the repetitive singsong of an Alzheimer's victim, I heard as her great thanksgiving for receiving anew the wondrous gifts of creation.

These summer rituals taught me profound lessons. I realized from Ann's twice daily thanksgivings for the same trees, flowers, views, birds, animals, clouds, and rocks she had seen only hours or minutes earlier that it is possible always to live in adoration. I learned to pause and to bless. And I became aware that when the ordinary links between past, present, and future are gone, the grace of the immediate remains.

During our walks, Ann restored to me capabilities I had often squandered: the ability to be still and accept each moment in its freshness; to step into the flow of God's fullness, beauty within beauty; to bless God in the here and now; and to pray a pure and simple, "Thank you."

❧

O God, whose nature is to fill all nature, keep me within the fullness of each present moment so that thanksgiving becomes my way of life. Amen.

11

HEART PRAYER

And all who heard it were amazed at what the shepherds told them. But Mary treasured all these words and pondered them in her heart. The shepherds returned, glorifying and praising God for all they had heard and seen.

St. Luke 2:18–20

While constantly caring for Ann, I noticed my prayers were said sometimes by rote, sometimes in frustration, sometimes in tears, and almost always they were interrupted. When I used familiar prayers—the Serenity Prayer, the Lord's Prayer, words remembered from the *Book of Common Prayer*—I experienced some comfort, but was not always sure I had prayed. I was not even certain that I knew anymore what prayer was.

In my efforts to understand the essence of prayer, I remembered Mary, the mother of Jesus, as someone who knew how to pray. The Magnificat (St. Luke 1:46–55), Mary's celebrated prayer of praise in response to her pregnancy, remains in Roman Catholic, Orthodox Christian, and Protestant Christian liturgies to this day. And countless faithful lift up their own prayers to Mary, that she might intercede on their behalf.

In considering the nature of prayer, it seemed to me that if anything might have driven Mary to her knees in prayer, it would have been the peculiar activities surrounding her parturition. In St. Luke's account, Mary had already heard from angels and conceived. Newly pregnant, she visited her cousin Elizabeth, who was in her second trimester; while there, Mary was moved to pray the Magnificat: "My soul doth magnify the Lord . . ." Six months later, she traveled with her fiancé, Joseph, from Nazareth to Bethlehem to register in the Roman tax census, as decreed by Caesar Augustus. In Bethlehem "she gave birth to her firstborn son and wrapped him in swaddling cloths, and laid him in a manger, because there was no room for them in the inn" (St. Luke 2:7).

As if that were not traumatic enough, now shepherds came tumbling into the stable to tell wondrous tales about an angelic appearance, a heavenly choir, and a promise of divine Shalom. All of this Mary treasured and pondered in her heart.

It is not recorded that in the midst of these puzzling, demanding circumstances Mary prayed. It is remembered, though, that she held these matters in her heart, perhaps intentionally hiding them from the rest of the world.

In St. Luke's story of Jesus' youth, Mary was again remembered to have "treasured all these things in her heart" (2:51). The twelve-year-old Jesus had been separated from his parents during the Passover festival in Jerusalem. Four days later they found him in the temple, astounding rabbis and elders with his understanding of Torah. Their family reunion was full of emotional contrasts: joy and anger, celebration and venting, gratefulness and confusion. Again, trauma and inner silence had come together.

These accounts of Mary and Jesus prompted me to reevaluate the nature of prayer. I knew that Mary's Magnificat derived from a Hebrew prayer ascribed to Hannah. In I Samuel 2:1–10 Hannah's poem of adoration was inserted into a story about the dedication to God of her miraculously born son, Samuel. Realizing this, I thought that perhaps all powerful prayers were connected to long-nurtured traditions and were spoken in words crafted and polished over generations. But as an ordinary individual, I certainly did not have the aid of generations or the help of saints and angels in composing beautiful prayers, even though I knew I had been visited by living saints who assisted with health care, and by angels who dwelt within whatever light flowed into the darkness of our days and nights. At the same time I also believed that the prayers of ordinary people *were* heard by God.

Moreover, the biblical accounts of prayer caused me to think the wondering and pondering I engaged in while caregiving may themselves have been acts of prayer. Perhaps the mounting confusion, accrual of pain, and growing uncertainty about my time with Ann had no better place to go than into the treasury of my heart. Perhaps my heart was a perfect house of prayer and my caregiving was building there a precious altar.

Although I could not be certain of these suppositions, I did know that whenever I acknowledged my heart's daily burden to be prayer itself, I felt my pain lifted to another place. It seemed to be a place where, like Mary's before me, a silent treasure quietly awaited the flow of angelic deliverance.

❧

O God, who makes the very silence ring with praise, hear my quiet, burdened heart as prayer, and grant me peace. Amen.

12

NO TIME FOR PRAYER

Devote yourselves to prayer, keeping alert in it with thanksgiving.

Colossians 4:2

As a caregiver I often sensed that in the midst of filled time there was no time. It was an odd sensation, because the continuum of activity also seemed endless. In fact, it *was* endless. The cycle of care moved forward so relentlessly that the only reality I could count on was that even the pauses between lost moments would be filled with the meeting of a need.

Early on, it became clear that there would be no time for me to attend to the quiet rhythms of personal prayer. Accustomed to the cadence of the *Daily Office*, the prayer book used by Episcopal clergy, I had become habituated to spending time apart from Ann in prayer. Now, as her caregiver, I could see there was certainly not going to be "time apart" from her. What a dilemma this was! I could sacrifice neither caring for Ann nor praying to God.

Fortunately, the problem was soon resolved. I had long believed that there is only one activity necessary in life: to adore God. The Gospels of Saints Matthew, Mark, and Luke each remember Jesus to have answered a question about how best to honor the competing demands of life with the simple assertion that the Shema of Israel (Deuteronomy 6:4, 5) summarizes all that God requires: "Hear, O Israel: the Lord our God, the Lord is One; you shall love the Lord your God with all your heart, and with all your soul, and with all your mind, and with all your strength." And yet God had given me another necessary activity—to be by Ann's side as Alzheimer's disease took her off into unknown places. Consequently, I reasoned that if there was to be *no* time for prayer, then *all* time would be spent in prayer.

Thus I began to reacquaint myself with the Russian Orthodox monastic "art of prayer"—the constant repetition, in the presence of God, of a single phrase—a practice known today as "breath prayer." Whenever I thought of Ann, which was almost constantly, I would lift up my prayer: "For God alone, my soul in silence waits" (Psalm 62:1). Whenever I thought of need, worry, future, fear, medications, up went the prayer, which quickly became part of my life.

Being in unceasing prayer was initially difficult, an issue I addressed through simple activities. For example, when Ann felt comfortable sitting outside in the sunshine, I would split wood to the rhythm of my prayer. I also prepared food and fed Ann in rhythm with my prayer. Eventually, the prayer moved from my lips to my mind and then into my soul. I recall the night I awoke by Ann's side to discover that I was in the middle of the prayer. It was then I knew that the prayer was praying me!

This constant repetition did not replace other forms of prayer. Instead, it became a context for all my other praying— much like the drone in a sitar and tabla concert, where string and drum rise and fall against the constancy carrying the fluid melody. For me, breath prayer became the drone and vehicle for all other strains of prayer.

As I continued in my caregiving, the phrase I lifted up in prayer was most helpful. It needed no answer; it revealed God's mercy; and it became a constant soft reminder of God's healing presence in my life with Ann and her illness.

∞

O God, who reaches within me with my every breath, so fill my breath with prayer that I might be constant in my devotion. Amen.

13

GOD'S PRAYER

During his life on earth, Jesus offered prayer and entreaty, aloud and in silent tears, to the one who had the power to save him out of death, and he submitted so humbly that his prayer was heard.

Hebrews 5:7

As difficult as it was to serve Ann's needs and God's devotion simultaneously, I slowly began to integrate them into my daily rhythms. Nonetheless, there were times when I questioned my ability to carry on. When Ann would ask over and over for the same information—"Who is coming today? Why? When? Who is she, anyway?"—I feared my own senses might leave me in my repetitive answers to her.

How could I give form to my prayers, even my breath prayer, if my soul energy was fixed on the tasks at hand? In struggling with this dilemma, I began to sense that praying while in the unrelenting grip of caregiving was ultimately shaped by God, and as I became aware of lifting up my powerlessness to God, I also began to experience how God lived in the cries and tears of prayer.

I came to realize that the assurance I felt came not from some "answer" but instead from God's involvement in prayer. In the restless days and ravaged nights of praying while caregiving, I knew that I was not merely a supplicant praying to a God who was already fully aware of my sorrow, but rather a participant in God's own prayer life.

My human prayer was formed within the heart of the Holy One—not simply *lifted* there, but *born* there. Just as I was held in the heart of God by the prayers of others, so was I being shaped in prayer. Thus I began to believe that the stream of prayer *to* God was ultimately *of* God.

The author of the Hebrews passage suggests that Jesus at prayer is the primary model for praying, because in Jesus, God is at prayer. Moreover, he voices God's humility before the powers of evil and death as well as God's awe in the presence of the even greater powers of goodness and renewal. This verse suggested to me that through God's prayer, offered "aloud and in silent tears," my sorrow was hallowed, and that everything in my realm of experience was in God's realm of experience. As a result, God's cries and tears began to touch the pulse of my mourning.

I felt like I was being welcomed into a cosmos of adoration, in which my prayers were being bound up with God's, much as Jesus' had been. Jesus, I knew, had also prayed in solitude (St. Luke 5:16, 6:12), even during his lonely hours in Gethsemane (St.

Luke 22:41). There, as Hebrews 5:7 indicates, Jesus' personal will was woven into God's will with finality and grace.

My Gethsemane was by Ann's side. I wondered if my passion could become as clarified and purified as Jesus'. Listening to the peace of God, I began to think of my powerlessness as the power of God to *feel* with me. God's empathy, I concluded, was not locked up in the events of Holy Week, but rather was an eternal prayer for deliverance. I was being invited both to identify holiness with suffering and to partner with God in prayer. Previously, I had been able to remember prayers and praying, but this was like "re-membering" my life in prayer in harmony with God's own.

Shifting my perspective in this way helped me feel more confident in prayer. Soon I was praying not simply *to* God but *with* and *within* God—a grace I might not have come by without the exhaustion of caregiving.

I came to believe God was also weary of the demands of illness, dementia, and dying, and was simply waiting for me to accept the invitation to become one with divine prayer. Mercifully, I was lifted up to a loving place where cries and tears from the heart of terror were joined with God's passion. Rather than reject my powerlessness before the incomprehensible evil of Alzheimer's disease, God magnified it by joining it with the heart of the divine.

ᘒ

O God, whose prayer it is that I be with You in prayer, prepare my heart to pulse with Your own, that my cries and tears be one with Yours. Amen.

14

PRAYERS IN THE DARK

Where can I go from your spirit? Or where can I flee from your presence? If I ascend to heaven, you are there; if I make my bed in Sheol, you are there.

Psalm 139:7, 8

One day when I was reading to Ann from what turned out to be her last beloved book, I became abruptly aware of her utter lack of comprehension. Ann's favorite genre was biography, and I had been reading an account of Eleanor Roosevelt's life to her for some time. On this occasion I was shocked to learn that Ann had lost her ability to understand the meaning of words from this realm of writing that had meant so much to her.

In that moment I felt as though I had entered the darkness and silence of Sheol with her. Psalm 139, however, elevated my adoration of God to a new level of devotion. For here was a fresh confession: those who go down into Sheol are still in the presence of God. Further along in Psalm 139, I was reassured that "If I say, Surely the darkness shall cover me, and the light around me become night, even the darkness is not dark to you;

the night is as bright as the day, for darkness is as light to you" (11, 12).

So it was that while stumbling around in the gloom of Sheol, my sights were lifted. Each time I feared I had made my bed in Sheol, I prayed this new, bright profusion of blessing: "You are there. You are there."

In celebrating God's pervasiveness by professing the "ancient way" (24) of remembering God's eternal presence in all creation, Psalm 139 reminded me that prayer was a means of traveling to God's dwelling place. Thus prayer became my acceptance of God's invitation to be with a holy presence everywhere. I came to believe that prayer was like touching eternity.

When I felt God's hand upon me like that, I would also think about the spiritual dimension of Ann's slow, demented dying. Her diminishment, I realized, was like my prayer, for she, too, was brushing against the eternal; her remembering, knowing, and willing were being replaced by a great quiet. What had been familiar to her in space and time was now unfamiliar. The landscape was melting away, and the ordinary reference points of home, family, work, friends, and special places seemed to be converging into a misty shroud of silence.

Eventually, I was comforted by this new thought: if the psalmist could stand everything on its head and passionately claim that God gathers up all reality, perhaps I, too, could make a bold new claim. The psalmist's poetic proclamation that there is no place from which God's spirit is absent freed me to look at Ann's illness as a way of stepping into God's eternal presence. The psalmist encouraged me to think of my prayer and Ann's suffering alike as openings into God's infinite care.

While trying to understand what was happening to Ann as her dementia and loss deepened, I had learned something startling: her *soul* was not dying or fading into nothingness. The psalmist's words reminded me that God, the Eternal One, attended Ann's journey. Yes, Ann was losing time and space, but not to the void of nowhere. I could now hold Ann before God in prayer as a living soul capable of experiencing the comfort of the Divine Presence, as one who was entering the doorway to eternity.

I began to ask myself, could it be that, as mystics of all spiritual traditions suggest, one's loss of time and space is really a foreshadowing of an entry into the eternal? Even without the assurance of an answer, I felt much better prepared to move on to the next aspect of caregiving when I saw Ann as an angel of light rather than a harbinger of darkness and silence.

I prayed that this perception might be so—that Ann was treading softly on God's good ground, that her soul was brushed by the wings of eternity, that she was exploring the touch of God's presence in both heaven and Sheol, and that what I saw so darkly was really her bright light with God.

☙

O God, who dwells everywhere I go with my mind and body, who is there before me and beyond me, keep me and my loved one tenderly in Your presence. Amen.

ON THE FAMILY OF GOD

15

HOLY DESPAIR

Eli, Eli, lema sabachthani? My God, my God, why have you forsaken me?

Psalm 22:1 and St. Matthew 27:46

I remember the precise moment it occurred to me that the place spread before Ann in her dementia had been cleansed by God. It was in the midst of a particularly trying day. Bathing, dressing, and feeding had been clumsy, and we were both in despair. Then suddenly I saw the presence of God in my crazed and demented love.

I saw God broken, and I understood in a flash that the ninth-hour cry of Jesus from the cross was the psalmody of the demented. Ann's illness had brought me to my knees, and here I had found a place where God had preceded her in her suffering. I remembered Golgotha, Place of the Skulls, outside Jerusalem, where shocked believers had heard Jesus' piercing cry—the opening line of a Davidic psalm sung to the tune "Doe of the Dawn."

Everyone within earshot at Golgotha would have recognized this anthem of distress. Still, mockery reigned. The silly conjecture that Jesus had called on Elijah only added to the moment's bitterness. It is not written that Jesus chanted the entire psalm; what is recorded is that Jesus felt forlorn, that he had touched dementia and hopelessness. And this was what I needed to remember. Thus with my new view of despair, I lingered on this biblical passage and did not hasten to the happy ending of Psalm 22 and its message of delivery and joy.

To confront Alzheimer's disease is to deal with fragmentation and debilitation. Yet I experienced healing while focusing on Jesus' feelings of incapacitation and disconnectedness. In this instant he was brutally torn from mind, heart, and soul—enough to dementedly lament that God had forsaken him.

While imagining God's heart and love crushed by evil, I was deeply touched. What it meant for me was that the terrible ground on which Ann and I stood had been made holy and the company Ann kept in her debilitation was with God. My loved one had been robbed of vision, understanding, community, and imagination—just as in one moment God had been.

I could see that nothing in Alzheimer's disease remained untouched by God's cleansing rage and that Ann's illness was redeemed by God's purifying presence and blessed by God's bitter tears. With this realization, I felt the fullness of God's presence moving through my life joy by joy, agony by agony. I was the one who remained to remember God. Ann, in her lost space and bewildered time, would no longer be coming back to the familiar. Yet in her presence I had been delivered by grace to Golgotha where, miraculously, God had stepped into those lost, dark places and blessed them.

∾

O God, whose desire it is that no lost way be deprived of Your love and care, seize my breaking heart, heal me with Your presence, and lead me back to holy ground. Amen.

16

MOUTHS OF BABES

At that same hour Jesus rejoiced in the Holy Spirit and said,
"I thank you, Father, because you have hidden these things
from the wise and the intelligent and have revealed them to
infants; yes, Father, for such was your gracious will."

St. Luke 10:21

One lovely sunny summer afternoon my four-and-a-half-
year-old granddaughter Elizabeth Ann and I were visiting
Ann, her beloved Granny, at Namasté. This was not the first
time Elizabeth had visited her Granny there, but it was the
first time she had come unaccompanied by her parents, aunts,
and uncles.

Ann, now in her fourth month at Namasté, had lost inter-
est in speaking and in group activities, maintained no eye contact, and seemed beyond our reach. Nevertheless, Elizabeth
and I took her for a walk through the large dayroom and out

onto the peaceful grounds toward a duck pond. Along the way we gave Ann news of family and friends. About twenty minutes into our slow walk, Elizabeth, holding Ann's left hand while I gripped her right arm, turned to me and said, "Grandpa, will you please go away now. I want my own private time with Granny." Stunned by her request, I helped Elizabeth seat her Granny on a bench by the pond, and then retreated.

From about fifty feet away, I watched them through tears of joy and pain. Elizabeth was animated: she held her Granny's face in her small hands and looked her straight in the eye, pranced before her with poise and grace, showing off her new hair ties, and snuggled onto her Granny's lap. The smile on Ann's face glowed with radiance.

Later in the day, I asked Elizabeth what she had talked about with Granny during their private time together. She gave me one of her learned-from-Granny incredulous looks and said, with due emphasis on the drama of the moment, "Well, *Grand*pa, when I was hugging and kissing her, I wasn't talking about *any*thing. I was just loving her!"

From the innocent heart of my granddaughter I had now learned how to articulate my brush with the family of God. In my weary journey as a caregiver, I had known that Ann and I were engaged in an intimacy of wonder far surpassing anything I had ever experienced in our long relationship. During prayer and meditation, however, I had increasingly been led to the harmony and union of the family of God. In times of great distress I would imagine the light of this family raying out into the mist of my suffering. Yet, too timid to talk about this image, I held it quietly in my heart, not knowing if its seed would ever germinate in my soul.

Now the soil had suddenly broken and the flower of my imagining was in full bloom. The invitation to participate in holiness while wending my way through these ragged days had come in the form of this tender interchange between Elizabeth and Ann. Precious freedom and hope within God's family was mine for the claiming. Seizing the moment, I accepted the invitation—spurred on not by my adult wisdom, but by a child's spontaneous act of love.

Surely, the ground on which Ann and Elizabeth loved each other that awesome afternoon had been made holy by God's precious touch. And God's large, caring family had with open arms embraced the hurt in our small family.

∾

O God, as You speak in the hearts of children from the depths of Your own heart, help me always to live as fully as I can within Your family of care. Amen.

17

THE PLACE OF DEATH

For this is the reason the gospel was proclaimed even to the dead, so that, though they had been judged in the flesh as everyone is judged, they might live in the spirit as God does.

I Peter 4:6

During my pilgrimage with Alzheimer's disease, I spoke with many of Ann's dear friends. Always, we would talk about the horrible pathos of the great lost space to which she—a once bright, insightful, witty, liberated woman—had retreated. Sometimes these conversations served to massage a false hope into Alzheimer's heinous consequences. Then, while sharing our grief, there usually came a mighty realization: our words had no magical power to change reality, but simply wrapped our hearts in sadness and bewilderment.

What often followed was an expression of compassion extended my way, such as: "It must be terrible for you. How awful to see Ann so debilitated. How do you manage? What can I do?" Having learned to be honest about my deep sense of loss, I would reply, "It is worse than death."

During an intense conversation with Jean, one of Ann's most compellingly spiritual friends, this despairing view of Alzheimer's disease shifted. Many months earlier, while out for lunch one day, Ann and I had told Jean of the diagnosis, whereupon she had slapped her fists on the restaurant table and shouted for all to hear, "Oh, *shit!*"—eliciting my first lesson in holy rage and sacred anger. Now Jean was saying, with tear-rimmed eyes and flushed cheeks, "But how can it be? If this is worse than death, what are we to do?" The despondency in her voice indicated that the threads of her usually constant faith were about to unravel.

Just hours before, Jean and I had worshiped together with other clergy and family members, using the quiet cadences of the *Book of Common Prayer*'s Daily Morning Prayer. There we had confessed our tottering faith through the ancient words of the Apostles' Creed, uttering the phrase "descended into hell." Now linking my "worse than death" response with visions of hell, I saw that although Alzheimer's disease did increase my exposure to turmoil and destruction, it did not catapult me into a realm darker than death. I further realized that my slow walk beside Ann had *seemed* worse than death because we had ventured into the region of death without having died. Here shadows dominated the sparse light, and I could imagine life only as a vague semblance of what it had been. But in conversation with Jean I was able to see that this dreaded realm did indeed have its glory, that in deep dusk there is an abiding light.

I had never imagined there would come a time in my life when one of the strongest assurances I found in my faith was also one of the strangest. Yes, I concluded, God has swept in peace through all the places of death, even this place of death where Ann lives.

Even though Jean and other friends still had tears and rage, and I continued to feel exhaustion and grief, I was grateful to know that God had boldly brooded before me in this twisted place of death. God had hallowed this ground that threatened to remain unhallowed, and had brought good news to the festering gloom of hell.

∽

O God, within whose reach lies all my living and all my dying, so strengthen me in my vision of Your love that I may walk boldly with You and my loved one in the hallowed places of death. Amen.

18

CONFUSION AND GLORY

While Jesus was still speaking to the crowds, his mother and his brothers were standing outside, wanting to speak to him. Someone told him, "Look, your mother and your brothers are standing outside, wanting to speak to you." But to the one who had told him this, Jesus replied, "Who is my mother, and who are my brothers?"

St. Matthew 12:46–48

Ann would wander through our home at night, usually in the darkest predawn hours, looking for her deceased father. During the day, she would introduce me as her son, her sons as her brothers, and mix the identity of her daughters-in-law with great abandon. For Ann, the hard edges of personal identity had softened, blurring her sense of family. We who loved her did not correct her, for as far as we were concerned, she had the right to name us as she wished, the freedom to claim what she could of her world—in her own terms and with dignity.

Still, I was often tempted to rectify Ann's perceptions of reality. My obsession with accuracy seemed to have arisen from the insecurity I felt living in the topsy-turvy world of Alzheimer's disease. Because of the pain and uncertainty involved in witnessing Ann's diminishment, I fantasized setting the world aright by calling up all the original referents: "No, your father is dead," "No, I'm Wayne," "No, these are your sons, Christopher, Peter, and Gregory," "No, this is Dasha, not Mary."

Addressing my fear by admonishing Ann, however, would only have frustrated and shamed her. Nonetheless, it hurt to enter Ann's world and to follow her on the meandering path she cut through the once familiar. It hurt all the more each time I recalled Ann saying there would come a day when she would no longer recognize those she loved. Now this day had come.

In my efforts to refrain from correcting Ann's confused reality, it helped to remember that Jesus had also turned family identity upside down, redefining these relationships in broader terms, as in the passage from St. Matthew quoted above. Thus it was not only dementia that so innocently wreaked havoc with life—it was also holiness. Moreover, Jesus was surrounded by people who wanted reassurance of his true identity and their relationship to him: "Is not this Jesus, the son of Joseph, whose father and mother we know?" (St. John 6:41); "Is not this Joseph's son?" (St. Luke 4:22); "Is not this the carpenter's son? Is not his mother called Mary?" (St. Matthew 13:55); "Is not this the carpenter, the son of Mary?" (St. Mark 6:3).

In trying to cope with the pain of being misidentified by Ann, I considered what Mary might have experienced when Jesus asked publicly, "Who is my mother?" He went on to define his mother and family as those who were as on fire with Torah as he was, and who heard Torah from him and lived it.

Like Mary before me, I felt the pain of being excluded from warm, familial regard. Both Mary and I had been wounded by displacement: she had been denied as mother, and I as husband. But as I churned through my feelings about living in a family remade by dementia, I held my center by remembering that the holy was also a place where great undoings were woven into wonderful new fabrics.

While wandering the night with Ann and entering into her world of place, time, and identity, I thought about this strange mixture of the sacred and the demented. Yes, I was sad and distressed that Ann was slipping away from my world, but at the same time, I smiled in bittersweet recognition of how the holy invades what we consider reality with abandon, erraticism, and grace. Although I wished I could have been introduced to the holy in less harsh ways, I came to see this, too, as the way of the sacred

❧

O God, who fills all time and space with glory, open my eyes to the holy that I might play with wonder in my days and nights of sorrow. Amen.

19

THE TWIN IN US

Thomas, who was called the Twin, said to his fellow disciples,
"Let us also go, that we may die with him."

St. John 11:16

The apostle Thomas Didymus is usually remembered
through a story in the twentieth chapter of St. John, in which
he earned the epithet "doubting Thomas." The events took
place after reports of Jesus' resurrection:

> But Thomas (who was called the Twin), one of the twelve,
> was not with them when Jesus came. So the other disci-
> ples told him, "We have seen the Lord." But he said to
> them, "Unless I see the mark of the nails in his hands, and
> put my finger in the mark of the nails and my hand in his
> side, I will not believe" (St. John 20:24–25).

A week later Jesus stood among them all once again and invited Thomas to "put your finger here and see my hands. Reach out your hand and put it in my side. Do not doubt but believe" (St. John 20:27).

Despite the fact that Thomas doubted, he was also considered courageous, brave, and loyal, according to a story in the eleventh chapter of St. John. Here Thomas, alone among the disciples, is remembered for his bold insight into the personal and political consequences of Jesus' teaching and healing.

In the middle chapters of St. John, a politically charged account of Jesus' life, the tension mounts toward a climax of arrest and death. When Jesus made the momentous decision to cross back over the River Jordan into Judea, only Thomas affirmed it. He knew this journey would take Jesus into Jerusalem for the last week of his life. It was the Twin who said, "Let us also go, that we may die with him." So it seems there were two dynamics operating in Thomas.

While caregiving, I found it helpful to focus on Thomas's two dynamics since I also moved back and forth between courage and doubt, loyalty and despair. Here was a brother who had looked into the face of death and had chosen to go on that journey with the one he loved just as I had opted to accompany Ann in her struggle. When faced with Ann's impending death, I often saw myself as both a doubter and a hero. When weary and hopeless, sometimes I chose as my ally the feisty, demanding, cynical, doubting Thomas. Other times I identified with the twin who served as a model of faith—the feisty, demanding, believing, heroic Thomas.

During Ann's final silent days, I held the hollows of her temples and told her I saw the glory of her death nearby. I believe the Twin must have stood with me in those moments of farewell. While one part of me pulled back in despair and incredulity, crying, "No!" another part of me that wanted to die with my beloved was crying out with courage, "Let me also go!"

Had I not been able to cry out these words with hope and daring during my death walk with Ann, I might not have been able to feel the family of God in later days. When I was exhausted at the end of the journey, there remained this affirmation: after all my heroics were depleted, God's healing presence was still there.

∾

O God, whose way with me is constant, be present to my swings of mood and revive my tiring energies that I might walk again with You and my beloved. Amen.

20

AN OPEN DOOR

After this I looked, and there in heaven a door stood open!

Revelation 4:1

I was dumbfounded by the rapid progression of Ann's illness. I waited for some heavenly vision of healing, but to no avail. Futilely, I looked into the vacant place where my beloved lived, yearning for a welcoming door to appear, opening onto a different, more peaceful space.

Finally, I realized there were modest epiphanies that gave me great joy: a smile of recognition lighting up Ann's face; a phrase or name shining out of the sea fog like a beacon's light on the shore; a desire Ann would momentarily show for some activity from a past repertoire; a pause in the midst of daily needs to express joy from a place that had once been vibrant for her. Such moments were indeed like the longed for door opening to heaven, for they provided a piercing glance into the golden sunlight of Ann's former healthy presence. How divinely bright a moment it was when Ann's "Thank you" or "I love you" bubbled up delightedly from her lost language! I would think, this *is* heaven, for it magnifies into eternity a simple expression of grace and goodness from the here and now.

It was painful for me to exercise skills that had been stolen from Ann. I was still gifted with a here and now that meshed with my memories, hopes, and will, whereas the here and now Ann experienced was disconnected from her past and future. Yet it was my ability to experience love and thanksgiving in the flow of time that enabled me to receive the vision of heaven's door when it swung open during moments of caregiving.

Like the vision described in the fourth chapter of Revelation, there emerged on the other side of the door ajar to heaven the one thing necessary to sustain my life: adoration. When the door opened, no matter how briefly or narrowly, it gave cause for Eucharist and devotion. And even though, in contrast to the vision of Revelation, I did not see carnelian, rainbows, emeralds, thrones, golden crowns, crystal, and choirs, what I did see was just as splendid—single, simple moments of connection to the familiar. I was swept into adoration and praise precisely because of those moments.

Consequently, I began to think of heaven as the place where adoration never ceases, the state where praise and thanksgiving are no longer interrupted by the here and now. I realized that the door standing open to heaven really did open onto the known. Moreover, I came to believe that the characteristic following us to heaven will be the God-given ability to adore, love, and commune with light, wisdom, and goodness.

While these wonders sometimes brought me peace, other times they increased my pain. But my varying reactions did not matter. It was simply so, within the family of God and the reach of God's caring, that every once in a while, weary as I was, a door stood open to the bright welcome light of God's presence and healing. At such times I saw into the heart of God. What followed these isolated moments was the sense of a blessed goodness well beyond my pain and Ann's suffering.

∽

O God, who wills that heaven appear in my weariness, alert my eyes, that I might see when You gently open the door before me. Amen.

21

SHALOM

For God is a God not of disorder but of peace.

I Corinthians 14:33

The confusion and tumult I experienced during my final days of caregiving were extremely disorienting. They reminded me of the chaos St. Paul wrote of in his letters to the Corinthian churches, although his concerns were much different from my own. He was dealing with a squabbling congregation, while I was confronting at-home Alzheimer's care. But we were both doing something similar—sorting out, with as much wisdom as God gave us, the demands of daily living.

In addition to grappling with the concerns of caregiving, I was dismayed that the symptoms accompanying Ann's decline into dementia began to appear in *my* behaviors. Whatever Ann needed I turned to at once with a sense of urgency; if she searched for a word or a name, for example, I, too, immediately focused on the quest, no matter where my own thoughts were headed. The pleasure Ann sought I was quick to provide, regardless of what I might have been doing at the time. Moreover, living in the midst of Ann's confusion, I would sometimes turn from one thing to the next without any sense of how they were connected. These behaviors, mirroring her own, often had an unsettling effect on me.

At the same time, I provided order for Ann, although it was only a small bulwark against the great ocean of disorder surrounding us. I created structure for her security and safety, aware that it was only a tiny fortress on the war-torn plain of this chaotic disease. Often, I was comforted by St. Paul's recognition that God's character stood in opposition to chaos and confusion. Obviously, that quality in God was much more powerful than my meager, hopeful ordering of time, place, and objects. Still, St. Paul's words encouraged me to relate my small behaviors to the loving care of the God of peace.

Consequently, I began to associate God's peace with serenity and centeredness in the topsy-turvy world I lived in with Ann. When I was able to, I used occasions of weariness and mental confusion to focus, however briefly, on God. To live even for a single moment with God was to exist in stillness and peace. Although at times I could not fathom how my disordered and stressful life as a caregiver related to my life with God in these intervening moments of serenity, with the gift of faith I was eventually able to see that neither of these lives excluded the other.

That insight provided hope. If life with God were to exclude my fractured, worn days with Ann, or if my life as caregiver were to keep me from the good graces of God, then God would have remained hidden from me. Fortunately, neither was true.

The truth was that in the realm of chaos, God's peace was pervasive. And in my ragged disorder and confusion, opportunities gracefully arose for touching the God of peace. Sometimes I had thought the phrase "god of disorder" aptly described the hateful power of Alzheimer's disease. But St. Paul's pastoral reminder that God is a God of peace guided me toward the still place of divine care and serenity. Thus the insight St. Paul discovered in his own disquietude was healing for me: God is not a God of confusion, but of peace.

∽

O God, who is peace and who creates peace, lovingly lead me into a serene place with You, even when I feel confused in caring for my beloved. Amen.

EPILOGUE

In T.S. Eliot's *Murder in the Cathedral*, Thomas Beckett says, "I am not in danger, only near death." So it was for Ann. Neither Ann nor I were in danger, even though we walked with God near death.

After Ann had been at Namasté for two months, I brought her home to celebrate her fifty-ninth birthday. It was to be the first and last time we had a visit like that. I picked her up at Namasté in midmorning on a soft, gray day, and we quietly drove the sixty miles of plains, canyons, and forest to our mountain home. The first thing Ann said as we approached the house was, "I don't remember any of this."

I prepared one of her favorite lunches, a rich toasted vegetarian sandwich. Afterward, as we cleared the table and washed the dishes, Ann asked me where Wayne was, and would I please take her home. In those final moments together in our delightful bright house, I felt profoundly the larceny and violence of this wretched Alzheimer's disease.

As we left the house together for what would be the last time, Ann began to speak to me in the repetitious manner of Alzheimer's victims, telling me again and again that Wayne would be waiting for her at home or that Wayne was undoubtedly ahead of us in that car just beyond the next hill. And she repeatedly said to me, "I don't know who you are, but I know you are my friend."

During this confused final time together in our home, that was who I was for Ann: a person just over the next hill, a person waiting at home, a friend. All I could do was cherish the safety Ann experienced on the outing, and mourn this last passage from being known to being unknown. I was painfully aware that this was to be my last physical journey with Ann from the familiar to the alien, and that a boundary had been crossed where I passed from being safe lover to safe stranger.

In the gaps of silence during the afternoon's drive back to Namasté, however, a subtle shift in perspective helped me realize that it was not necessary to measure our life with Alzheimer's disease as a series of last acts. I had been accustomed to remembering, for example, the last time we planned and implemented a trip together, shared a hearty laugh, made love, bought a gift for one of our children, and so on. Now, instead, I could choose to look at firsts: the first time I dressed Ann, tucked her into bed, shampooed and blow-dried her hair, walked through the night with her in quest of her dead father; became simply her new friend on a gray day's drive through the mountains. Soon I began to cherish these firsts at least as much as I had mourned the lasts.

I gained another important insight during our drive back to Colorado Springs after Ann's birthday lunch. Only a short distance from Namasté, Ann turned from the fleeting scenery, looked at me for some time, then said quietly, "Everything is too large today. Everything is too large." With this astonishing admission, she opened a window onto her Alzheimer's experience. What for me were ordinary landmarks of a day were for Ann a burden of conversation, scenery, and blasted memory. I believe it was a gift for Ann, in her illness, to have been able to name the reality of her diminishment. For me this was a profound gift, imparting an opportunity to experience life through her senses.

This revelation was also a first—the first time she had confided to me, now a friendly stranger, the reach of her disease into the features of time and space I so blithely took for granted. Ann had won her way in life as a truth-teller, and she told the truth to the end.

Ann died, quietly and peacefully, a little more than four months after her sixtieth birthday. Although she had not made it intact to the end of her life, she died a death few of us have the honor of achieving—she died publicly, attended to with grace, dignity, and compassion.

Ann's passage into the glory of death was not a tragedy. Her death was welcome, serene, and liberating. The tragedy for Ann, family, and friends had been the disease itself. Now that, too, had passed away. In the end what had seemed like a disease of the soul had really been an education in the *wisdom* of the soul. Ann's soul, although quieted, had become nourishment for my own, opening me to the powers of God above, beyond, and within all life and death.

Finally, after all the farewells, there was one noble welcoming of the new: the restoration of my own memory and truth in the arms of God. I could not have traveled the paths I had taken had not God's presence infused the journey. I once thought in the dark nights of soul that my resources were finite and Alzheimer's was infinite. Yet I came to know just the opposite was true: this savage disease was finite, and my resources infinite. For even though in confronting this disease my physical energies were limited, I had within my grasp the infinite soul capacity to walk into Sheol and see that God was there.

I also learned, after these years of studying and meditating on Jewish and Christian scriptures, that there really is a focused biblical perspective on life, and that it nourishes fearlessness. Moreover, while both in the crucible of pain and in lighter times of joy, I realized it was possible to *choose* to live without fear. Scripture pointed the way to the solace I needed as a caregiver, and in following its lead I discovered only one thing is necessary, and that is to adore God—all else is choice.

Despite my weary body, broken heart, and confused mind, I was still free to choose to step with Ann as she walked with God. I was free to be present to the holy with silence and union. I was free to listen through my pain and loss to the whispers of eternity while time and place dropped away. I now rest in the assurance that both Ann and I were healed; Ann simply happened to die.

I pray with you daily . . .

POSTLUDE

ALZHEIMER'S SEASONS

While I am with her in winter,
snow holds cold against
the window of our day,
ice and light freeze
on the west panes,
a far sun's soft turn
plucks at each ponderosa;
words, few between us,
carry love's aching burden,
all the puzzling wonder,
all the chilling rage.
Not yet asking, "Why?"
in silence we list
long, weary answers.

Within our simple touch,
fingers brush against familiar skin,
eyes lock in urgent affection,
nothing wasted in our economy
of menaced desire, our passion
a treasure hid far beyond
this evil's reach.

All in the heart of knowing,
so painfully knowing,
there shall be no spring between us,
the summers are spent, and the falls
of glistening aspen now are far gone.

To have held the heat
of long and fragile love
in this hard-fisted winter
was the gift of angels
kissing with grace
our weak and smaller hands.

I shall now miss her
in repeated winter darkness,
and walk spring forever
in loss of her bloom,
and be still in summer's forest,

remembering for her
flowers' delights
and sun-drawn creatures,
and watch in the eternal fall
for the turning of her leaf
to quiet and to sleep.

SUGGESTED RESOURCES

The widest range of resources for Alzheimer's caregivers is available from the national offices of the Alzheimer's Association. Founded in 1980, the association works through a network of more than 200 local chapters and is the leading organization in the United States focused on Alzheimer's research, education, advocacy, and public policy issues. The association offers a Caregiver Kit—including a 20-minute videocassette titled *Caring for the Caregiver* and related print materials—as well as such publications as *Caregiver Stress: Signs to Watch For . . . Steps to Take* and *Respite Care Guide.*

For materials, information, and the location of the chapter nearest you, contact:

Alzheimer's Disease and
Related Disorders Association, Inc.
919 North Michigan Avenue, Suite 1000
Chicago, IL 60611-1676
Phone: 800-272-3900
Fax: 312-335-1110
Web site: http://www.alz.org

ILLUSTRATIONS

cover: Sunflower, Santa Fe, '97

frontispiece: Dr. Ann M. Ewing (early fall 1982)
        photo by Sally Kennedy
        photo illustration by Dasha Wright Ewing

page 14: Church of the Holy Sepulcher, Jerusalem, '97

    24: Mary's Well, Nazareth, '97

    52: Prayer at Western Wall, Jerusalem, '97

    78: Pacific Northwest Beach, Washington, '96

    102: Church of the Beatitudes, Israel, '97

    108: Mount Washington, Vermont, '95

All images have been produced by Dasha Wright Ewing unless otherwise noted.

ABOUT THE AUTHOR

WAYNE EWING, PhD, received his doctorate in theological studies from Yale University. His thirty-year professional life spanned college, university, and seminary teaching and administration in the United States and Singapore; private practice as a pastoral psychotherapist; parochial responsibilities as an Episcopal deacon and priest; journalism; and development of sustainable living practices in northern New Mexico. A published poet, he continues to write from his residence in San Carlos, Sonora, Mexico.

ABOUT THE PHOTOGRAPHER

DASHA WRIGHT EWING is a New York-based photographer who specializes in travel and food. Her photographs have appeared in a number of magazines, including *Elle Decor, Interior Design, New Woman,* and *New York.* This is her first book project.

ORDER FORM

Quantity	*Amount*
_____ *Tears in God's Bottle: Reflections on Alzheimer's Caregiving* ($23.00)	_____
Sales tax of 5% for Arizona residents	_____
Shipping & handling ($1.50; plus $.50 per book on orders of two or more)	_____
Total amount enclosed	_____

Quantity discounts available

Method of payment
❏ Check or money order enclosed (made payable to
   WhiteStone Circle Press in US currency only)
❏ MasterCard
❏ VISA   _____

         Expiration date _____

Signature _____

Please photocopy this order form, fill it out, and mail it, together with your personal check, money order, or charge-card information, to:

WhiteStone Circle Press
1718 East Speedway Boulevard, Suite 319
Tucson, AZ 85719
Phone toll-free: 877-424-7253
Fax: 011-526-226-1380